T.N.T.

IT ROCKS THE EARTH

CLAUDE M. BRISTOL

CONTENTS

FOREWORD

It was that period approaching the end of the second year of the great economic depression when hopefulness had almost vanished from business life, and everyone was overwhelmed with fear, that Mr. Claude M. Bristol, my close business associate of many years standing, astounded me by relating a most amazing experience in having found *"that something"* for which he had been searching many years.

As he revealed the truths which had come to him I, at first, was skeptical, but as he took me along with him, I, too, began to see the light which only stimulated my ambition for further knowledge of the theme of how to live powerfully by adopting that science which relates to the development of the human personality.

I realized that there was a great change for good coming over myself, and sensed the possibilities of what could be done if the members of our own organization put the author's teachings into practice, and forthwith arrangements were made for him to talk to our entire staff. The immediate response of every member of our organization in demanding a copy—followed by the most remarkable transformation of individuals and organization, brought home the positive conviction to me that the message contained in his theme was exactly what the world most needed, and that a great service could be rendered by publishing same for general distribution.

In "T.N.T.—It Rocks the Earth," you are told exactly how to acquire a wonderful secret, that Power, or whatever you wish to call it, which, when accepted and developed through a process of right thinking, creates a philosophy of life which sweeps away all obstacles and brings that which every human desires: success, happiness and contentment.

If it were not for the fact that I am intimately acquainted with the author I would pause to wonder where he acquired those facts and principles which he sets forth in his story, but suffice to say that I know that he knows what he is talking about, and he clearly outlines a system of mechanics which can be used by every one— irrespective of his or her walk in life.

Do exactly as he says, put his plan into operation—and I also promise you that almost overnight you will be transformed and the things for which you have wished all your life will be yours. Your fears, trials and tribulations will fade into the mists. The door of yesterday will be closed forever. A grand and glorious feeling will engulf you and you will smile, and when you do, the world will smile with you.

I know it. I believe it and it is so.

FRANK W. CAMP.

"There is no doubt in my mind that we will get in life what we desire in the ratio of the earnestness of our purpose in going after it."—J. C. PENNEY.

AUTHOR'S NOTE

To express the thought in another way: We get out of life exactly what we put into it— nothing more, nothing less. So it is with the message within these pages. You will get out of it in the same ratio which you accept the theme and apply the principles. Therefore, if you wish to develop and get what you want in life, do not loan or give this book away but make it your constant companion and reread it as frequently as possible. The more often it is reread the more workable become the principles and the clearer the road ahead.

DETONATING CAPS

"He who does not know what the world is does not know where he is. And he who does not know for what purpose the world exists, does not know who he is, nor what the world is." —A FIRST CENTURY MESSAGE

For those of you who seek to learn and make progress, I gently lay this in your laps. I do so without the slightest fear but that it will turn your world entirely upside down— bringing you health, wealth, success and happiness, providing you understand and accept.

Don't Misuse It

Remember T.N.T. is a dangerously high explosive so when you gather it closely, handle it gently.

Down through the centuries its power has destroyed those who sought to misuse it, therefore exercise great care that it is used only for good.

It can be proved by the teachings of the Bible, certain well established laws of physics, and last but not least, just plain common sense. Read and determine for yourself whether or not the proofs I offer stand by themselves.

Some of you may see only the spiritual side, others recognize the scientific truths, and still others may accept it as just a practical operating device to put you on the road to success. No matter—many know the truth and for you who will open your minds, the light will pour in with dazzling white brilliancy.

Feel in Your Pocket

I'm indebted to an old friend of mine, an expert on X-Ray and electrical high frequency apparatus, who, when I was a boy experimenting with electricity, put the first bit of powerful T.N.T. in my pocket. Then I didn't know what it was and didn't understand, but fortunately it has remained there all through the years. As I look back I realize why he didn't make me understand what it was. He believed in me and knew that when I was ready to accept it I would. It's taken nearly 30 years, during which time I sought up and down the highways, looking, seeking and searching for the Secret—T.N.T. All of the time there was some in my pocket—mine for the mere reaching. However, I've got a firm grip on it now and I will divide it graciously, knowing if used wisely it will blow away all obstacles and straighten out the road on which you've been wanting to travel all your life.

For many years I was a newspaperman and frequently I was behind the scenes. I met great men and women, interviewed famous people. Naturally I studied them and tried to understand what peculiar qualities they possessed that placed them above the others, but their secret evaded me.

Then came the war and I wondered why others made progress while I seemed to be "blocked" in my own ambitions. The war did teach me, however, that I could sleep in the mud, eat moldy bread and live to laugh about it. This is part of my T.N.T. so remember what I learned. It helped me to give old man Fear a solar plexus blow and I believe it will help you.

Hoping to find a royal road to fortune I read hundreds of the so-called "Success" books and they took me nowhere. I did the same with books on philosophy, psychology and still the great Secret kept just a jump ahead of me. I joined secret fraternal organizations, hoping that I might find that which I sought. However, just like the bit of T.N.T. in my pocket the Secret was in every book, in the great orders, everywhere, and in fact, right under my very nose but something kept me from it. You will have to determine for yourself what keeps you from it if you don't get it from T.N.T. It's there—if you don't find it in the printed word look between the lines—as I've done my best to present it to you.

Are You Afraid?

Following the war I became a member of a coast-wide investment banking organization and during the years I cherished quite a dream—as did thousands of others in all lines of business—only to discover that the air castles which I built were on an unstable foundation. That something which turned the world upside down financially entirely obliterated my air castles, and I became afraid. I got lost in the fog. Everywhere I turned something fell in on me.

As an executive of the organization my responsibilities multiplied. Our business, due to the economic changes which were taking place in the world, faced a crisis, and many people failing to understand the catastrophe which had overtaken business everywhere were critical. All of which brought worry and many sleepless nights. I found myself dreading to go to my work— fearing that each day would bring added misery. The weeks went on and conditions got worse and worse. I was baffled. Several times I talked about getting out of the business and one day in the latter part of June 1931, I made up my mind to leave. I mentioned it to one of the women with whom I had been associated for several years and saw nothing but reproach in her eyes. That night I tried to sleep. Again I found it impossible. I paced the floor for hours—when at about 3:30 in the morning I suddenly stopped and sat down. I was face to face with myself. I could follow the inclination to run and leave the others to carry on by themselves, or I could stay and do my share; a duty which I knew was mine. I caught myself saying almost aloud: *"Right is right. It's always been right. It can't be otherwise;"* something I had been taught since infancy.

Suddenly there appeared to be an unfoldment. Out of the air came a voice saying: *"What have you been seeking all these years? What were you taught? What did you learn? Where have you been? Where are you going?* I jumped to my feet crying: *"I know it. I've got it now. It's the secret. That's what they tried to teach you. It is the Royal Secret, too."*

Something told me that I would find those identical words in a book which had many years before been given me and which I had tried to read, failed to understand and put aside. It was written by a great man—Albert Pike—a mystic, a poet and a scholar. Grabbing it from the shelf, feverishly I ran through the pages. The words were there and I understood immediately.

Open Your Mind

I now had the key. I could see a broad smooth highway and at the end of that highway a perfect flood of gorgeously beautiful radiance. *"That's the road you are on now. What a simpleton you have been! They tried to teach you, they tried to help you and you kept your mind closed— thinking that you alone could find the road and stay on it."*

I was nearly overcome with the sheer joy of it all. My fears, my worries had disappeared. I smiled. I knew that I was right and that everything would be right for me from then on. I slept like a baby.

There was a different atmosphere in the office that day. The oppressive black clouds which hung over us began to fade away. I told the woman—she with the reproachful eyes—what had happened, and she smiled a knowing smile. She helped me get back on the track and I can never repay her.

As one learned man said: *"All of us are born with the ability to differentiate between right and wrong, and with the ability to achieve, but some of us must run head-on into a stone wall, smash ourselves to bits before we really know what it's all about."* I hit the wall with a terrific crash and it was the greatest and finest thing that ever happened to me.

Many noting the transformation asked for an explanation. I told some of my closest friends, and now it's for all of you because I know I can do good.

I keep the door of my private office open as I find I can do much for those who wish to talk with me.

The morale of our whole organization was at its lowest ebb. Everyone was discouraged. Afraid. By the very necessity of things we had to do an about-face.

Right Is Right

My job was doing everything I could to help the other fellow because I knew it was right. At first I was perplexed as to the methods I should employ to help them, but I used my own system in calling upon the subconscious, and the inner voice said that I should talk to them.

Some were skeptical, but I said to myself; "I can prove that I am right," and during the week that followed I spent every waking hour reviewing the books that I had studied through the years. Naturally the Bible came first; then followed studies in Yogiism, the philosophies of the old Greek and Roman masters and of the later day teachers and students. I again deliberated over the

Meditations of Marcus Aurelius Antoninus, reread Hudson's *Law of Psychic Phenomena, and* another book, *"The Gist of It,"* written by a brilliant physician, Haydon Rochester. Again I studied my books on physics, electricity and those on the vibrations of light and discovered that not only was I right, as I knew I would be, but that peculiarly the same general basic principles ran through them all. I reread numerous books on psychology and found the same story everywhere. Subsequently I quoted excerpts, and lo and behold, things began to move.

It has occurred to me again and again that all men and women who use this power are showmen, or to use the words of my newspaper days, headliners—those who hit the front page. Something causes them to toss away the bushel basket under which they hide their heads and they arise above the commonplace.

Where is Your Niche?

Surely you will agree that they may have the power to the Nth degree, but if they do not become headliners they never get a niche in the hall of fame. It doesn't follow that they are newspaper publicity seekers, because some of them are very reticent—and by their very reticence are showmen. Others adopt certain peculiarities or use certain devices to make them stand out from their fellowmen. Some wear an efficacious smile, others scowl—and still others have a certain charm of manner. Long hair, whiskers and sideburns play their part; flowing robes and distinctive dress are worn by others; the showmanship of some is evidenced by red neckties, others by spats, affected manners.

Many master the art of oratory, the science of warfare, banking, statesmanship, politics, the arts—but all of them stand out in the full glare of the calcium—headliners.

The number is legion. I mention a few of those of history and today: Desmosthenes, Nero, Julius Caesar, Christopher Columbus, Cleopatra, Balzac, de Maupassant, Sir Isaac Newton, Joan of Arc, Cromwell, Edgar Allen Poe, Benjamin Franklin, Alexander Hamilton, Bismark, Graham Bell, General Grant, Cecil Rhodes, P. T. Barnum, Clemenceau, Kitchener, Woodrow Wilson, Joffre, Sir Thomas Lipton, Foch, Mussolini,

Winston Churchill, Charles E. Hughes, Lloyd George, Mahatma Gandhi, Ramsey MacDonald, Will Rogers, Douglas Fairbanks, Herbert Hoover, Henry Ford, Lindbergh, Alfred E. Smith, Lenin and Hitler. They have been and are found in every walk of life.

Gandhi uses this power, I am sure, and I think he is the greatest headliner of present times. You can find many pictures showing him in the modern civilized garb of man, but today, and for several years he has kept his hair cropped short, worn a loin cloth and a pair of huge spectacles. I have no right to say that Gandhi affected this attire for any particular purpose, but I believe he has done it to focus the world's attention upon himself for India's cause.

We have seen Ely Culbertson, the bridge playing expert, perform. There have been few psychological devices that he hasn't used—he has "something"—and certainly no one can say he is not a headliner.

I make no attempt to explain why those who have this power are headliners. You'll have to determine that for yourself.

Detonating Caps are now set! Caution signals are out. Be Careful!

T.N.T.—IT ROCKS THE EARTH

"A man's true greatness lies in the consciousness of an honest purpose in life, founded on a just estimate of himself and everything else, on frequent self-examinations, and a steady obedience to the rule which he knows to be right, without troubling himself about what others may think or say, or whether they do or do not do that which he thinks and says and does."

—MARCUS AURBLIUS ANTONINUS.

There are thousands, yes, millions of people seeking the secret—the key to health, riches, happiness, contentment and a solution of their problems.

Through the ages many men and women had the secret, used the Power and I am positive you can acquire it too if you'll think as you read, accept and apply the ideas contained herein.

What do you want? Where are you going?

An Old, Old Story

I repeat an old story:

Down on a levee in Mississippi, two niggers were dozing—one of them yawned, stretched his arms and sighed: "Gee, I wish I had a million watermelons."

The other nigger said:

"Rastus, if you had a million watermelons, would you give me half of them?"

"No, sir!"

"Would you give me a quarter of them?"

"No, I wouldn't give you a quarter of them."

"Rastus, if you had a million watermelons wouldn't you give me even ten of them?"

"No, sir! I wouldn't give you ten of them."

"Well, wouldn't you give me one lousy watermelon?"

"Say, Sam, I wouldn't give you even a bite of one if I had a million watermelons."

"Why not, Rastus?"

"Because you're too lazy to wish for yourself."

There's much to be gleaned from that story. You'll understand as I proceed.

Scoffers Do Not Succeed

I am fully cognizant that some will scoff—there have always been scoffers, but scoffers never succeed. They never get any place in life—simply become envious, while the doer or the person who is moving forward has to jump over or go around them. They have nothing but a nuisance value in life. Some of you may dismiss all of this as you have done before—as you always will—but for those of you who are interested, are still willing to learn, I promise you can learn and make progress for yourself.

I take it there isn't an intelligent man or woman who isn't really interested in getting ahead, but I have often wondered if there isn't a negative quality in most of us which precludes us from really starting.

If You Believe It—It's So

There's a saying I thoroughly believe in: "If you believe it, it's so." Simply a cryptic statement or digest of what I give you. All the great teachers, Buddha, Confucius, Mohammed, Jesus and many philosophers taught a great fundamental idea. It is found in all religions, cults, creeds and sects. Everywhere runs the same general theme— the gist of which in my words is—"If you believe it, it's so."

I quote from the Bible: "As a man thinketh in his heart—so is he." *"As a man thinketh in his heart—so is he"—if you believe it, it's so.* Note the similarity? Reduce the whole thing to one word: *"faith."* I have heard many, many people say the day of miracles is past, but never in my life have I heard a thinker, a student or a believer make such a declaration. Surely, the days of Aladdin and his lamp are gone—perhaps they never existed—so with the magic wand, the magic carpet, and all of those things of fairy tale and legend.

Believe in Yourself

When I refer to miracles, I mean those things which can be accomplished through faith. Faith in your belief; Faith in Yourself; Faith in the persons with whom you are associated; Faith in a Power; Faith in That Something which controls the destinies of everyone—and, if you can get that Faith and dissipate the negative side, nothing in this world can stop you from acquiring what you desire.

While this may sound facetious, there is nothing you cannot have if you want it.

Why the Alibis?

All of us are prone to calculate and weigh things, permitting the negative side to creep to the fore, and our thoughts evidence themselves in such remarks as *"It can't be done;" "I'm afraid;" "What will happen if I do it?" "People won't understand;" "It isn't worth the effort;" "I haven't the time"* and similar verbal alibis. If you haven't expressed these thoughts to yourself, then others have to you, and, through the power of suggestion, you have accepted them as your own conclusions.

This same message has been written and delivered thousands of times. It runs through the Bible; you find it in the great fraternal orders; the crusaders carried it; every outstanding character of history has

used it; Moses, Alexander the Great, Napoleon, Shakespeare, Washington, Lincoln, Roosevelt, Wilson, Benjamin Franklin, Edison, Dr. Steinmetz,
Barnum, and thousands of others had a grasp of that something.

The Wise Men Knew

The wise men of all ages, the "medicine men," religious leaders, great teachers, the yogis, the "healers," the miracle men—all of them knew this secret. Some worked it one way—some another. They were just human beings. If they knew and could achieve, so can you.

Halt! Think! Ponder! What made Mussolini?

What is it that Aimee has? Gypsy Smith? Billy Sunday? Belief. Faith—only that, and the ability of a staunch believer to pass it on to the other fellow. It's the very keynote of all great religions. All big things are started by one person, one believer. It makes no difference where they got the idea originally. All great inventions are the outgrowth of the whole scheme—Faith. Faith—belief in yourself, your ideas. All super-salesmen know this—they use the Power—that's why they are super-salesmen. Every community drive, every forward movement, everything worthwhile succeeds because some one person has Faith and is able to pass it on and on and on. Think about that—then think about it some more, and think of it again. Meditate over it, and you'll realize that every word is true.

Don't Envy: Do

Many envy the man or woman getting ahead, who appears to be a financial success, a power, an influence. Did you ever seek the explanation? Everything that anyone has ever done constructively has been done from within himself.

Every one of us, if put on the right track, can accomplish what he or she is after by keeping before him or her my own expression: *"If you believe, it's so,"* and adopting the old adage: *"Where there's a will there's a way"*. In other words, get that willpower—that Faith—that Belief working every minute of the day—24 hours of the day—7 days a week—365 days a year. And I promise you if it's done you will leave people around you in the progress you make as rapidly as high frequency electrical discharges oscillate through the ether.

Stop! Think! Meditate!

Pause and think for a moment. What is organized propaganda? Nothing more, nothing less than a well developed plan to make you believe. You saw it work in the war days and if you're wide awake to what is going on around you, you know that it's being worked in every line of human endeavor today—just as it was worked thousands of years ago and as it always works. If you're reading the newspaper, listening to the radio and will keep in mind my theme, you will realize that all these speeches of our leaders, our great men coming to us with clock-like regularity are being given with a purpose—to make us believe. Those men know it works.

The Voice Speaks

Mahatma Gandhi upon arriving in England to seek a solution of India's problems said: *"I'm doing this because a voice within me speaks."*

Gandhi referred to *"something"* from within. Call it a Power, call it something supernatural, call it anything you wish. Some refer to it as the subjective mind. Others call it the subconscious mind; some instinct; still others to the impulses coming from within as hunches. Divine messages. Spiritualists refer to it as a voice from beyond. No matter what it is, it gets results, and now I show you how to acquire it.

Tap No. 1

First, however, permit me to set the stage by calling attention to the effect of repetition or reiteration. For example, take a pneumatic chisel—you have seen one used in breaking up solid concrete or piercing holes through steel. It's the tap, tap, tap, tap of that chisel with a terrific force behind which causes disintegration of the particles and makes a dent or hole in the object on which it is used.

All of us have heard of the old torture system of dripping water on the forehead. Perhaps you are familiar with Kipling's

"Boots." It's the tramp, tramp of boots, boots, that makes men mad. It's the constant never-ending repetition that penetrates.

You are familiar with the first part of the picture and how repetition works on material things, but some of you may not thoroughly understand the second part, but here, too, it's the repetition that ultimately makes its impression upon the human mind.

The fundamental of advertising is its repetition, its appeal by reiteration—*"It floats;" "There's a reason;" "I'd walk a mile;" "They're kind to your throat."* A hundred others all impressed on your mind by constant repetition—tap, tap, tap. Today our leaders are saying the same thing to us though perhaps in a different way. *"Have faith"; "Have courage"; "Move forward"; "Business is coming back",* etc. Repetition, reiteration—again and again. Tap, tap, tap.

The connection between the conscious and the subconscious or subjective mind is close. Every student of the subject knows what may be accomplished by definitely contacting the subconscious. If you can get a definite detailed picture in your conscious mind by using this process of reiteration or repetition and make the subconscious mind click, you have at your command a Power that astounds.

The Science of Suggestion

We hear much about the power of suggestion. We know how easy it is to make a person ill by constantly suggesting to him that he doesn't look well, etc. It's the constant mental review of his crime that suggestion makes a lawbreaker confess. As a newspaperman I have been in on many *"third degree"* sessions. I have seen detectives and prosecutors corner a single individual and shoot questions at that individual until his face was bathed in perspiration. It is the deadly repetition, the reiteration, the tap, tap, tap, through the power of suggestion which brings confession.

Skilled prosecutors, clever defenders appeal to the emotions of jurors, never to the conscious reason. And how do they do it? Simply by a process of repeating and emphasizing time after time the points they wish to stress. They do it with usage of words and variations of argument. Behind all there is that tap, tap, tap, tap—tapping—the subconscious—making the jurors believe.

If you will keep this idea of repetition in mind you will understand why the Jewish people are so successful in business. When families are gathered together, the subject of conversation is business, business. They talk their problems over—they keep before them constantly the idea of making money and making progress and never for a moment are they permitted to forget. And they stick together.

The idea there was born of necessity, just like a machine or an article is born of necessity. We are all familiar with the old adage, *"Necessity is the mother of invention"*—and it is true of all human impulses and endeavors. A drowning man grabs at a straw, a starving man at a crust of bread.

The impulses come when you get up against it. You who have been there know what you had to rely on in times of acute pressure, and whether or not you heard a little voice from within.

Where Are You Going?

There can be no gainsaying that once you have made up your mind to do a thing it will be done, but the trouble with most of us is that we sidestep, vacillate, and seldom make up our minds to what we want or determine clearly the road on which we wish to travel. All daydreams and wishes would become realities if we kept them constantly before us—put fear behind—shoved away all reservations, ifs, ands and buts. Again, a lot of us think we know what we want when, as a matter of fact, we don't. This sounds paradoxical but, if each of us knew what he wanted, he would get it, provided he had the willpower, the stamina, the dynamic force, the fight to go after it.

Therefore, the first thing to do is get that spirit of determination. That may be obtained by constantly saying to yourself —*"I will" "I will" "I will"* and *"I will"* and believe it. Then before you know it you will have developed a willpower which, coupled with these other things I am about to explain, will change your whole scheme of things and get you on the road to success. If you haven't the desire to improve your own individual position in life, then you had better stop reading right now and burn this.

However, if you have the desire, you are on your way to make progress.

What Do You Want?

No matter whether you be a salesman, an executive, a mechanic, a writer or what, or whether you are after money, love, improvement in social position, in the legal profession or medical profession, it makes absolutely no difference. You can utilize this power and acquire every single thing you want—whether it be a pair of shoes or a mansion.

Tap No. 2

Now if you have the desire, the foundation is laid. Get a perfect detailed picture of the exact thing, or things, you wish. If it is increased sales, fix the exact amounts; if it's something you want the other fellow to do for you, the love of a woman or the love of a man, a new suit of clothes or a new automobile—anything and everything. No matter what you are after under this system you can have it provided the desire is definite and positive.

He who knows how to plant, shall not have his plant uprooted;
He who knows how to hold a thing, shall not have it taken away.

—LAO TZU, THE CHINESE MYSTIC, 600 B.C.

Adopt This Tap System

When you have the picture firmly in mind begin using the tap, tap system as I have outlined. It is going to be the repetition, the reiteration of that picture upon the subconscious mind that will cause the little voice from within to speak and point out to you accurately and scientifically how you are to proceed to get what you want. And when you move all obstacles will become phantoms.

Use Small Cards

The idea is to keep the picture or pictures before you constantly. As an aid in the visualization of the things you want and to keep them uppermost in your mind, write a word picture of them on several small cards. (Election card size is convenient). Keep them always in your possession and look at them as frequently as possible—bearing in mind the more often you glance at them the firmer becomes the impression upon your consciousness. As a suggestion, pin one card above the mirror to be looked at in the morning when you shave. Permit the details of your wishes outlined on the card to increase as you continue to develop the mental picture. Have another card convenient to look at while you eat your lunch—your dinner. Use the cards again just before you go to sleep. Keep it up. Tap, tap, tap. However, there's no point to writing down your wishes until you have determined that every single detail of what you want is to be photographed permanently in your mind—to stay there until they become realities.

Where Is Your Mirror?

Augment the foregoing formula with the use of a mirror. Study yourself in the glass. Search deeply into your eyes. Become acquainted with yourself—know yourself thoroughly and have yourself tell yourself what you want and where you are going. Sooner or later you will see the reflections of your wishes in your mirror every time you peer into it—and your daydreams will gradually take shape. When you get the pictures clearly defined do not for an instant permit them to escape you. Hold them with bands of steel.

"So use all that is called Fortune. Most men gamble with her, and gain all, and lose all, as her wheels roll. But do thou leave as unlawful these winnings and deal with Cause and Effect, the chancellors of God. In the Will work and acquire, and thou hast chained the wheels of Chance, and shall sit hereafter out of fear of her rotations."

—EMERSON'S SELF-RELIANCE.

Constant practice of writing down your wishes and using a mirror will work wonders. Shortly you can form the pictures at will—without the use of either cards or mirrors—and you will find yourself tapping the subconscious mind almost automatically.

Start Wishing

Don't be afraid of over-doing, or becoming extravagant with your wishes and desires because, as I said before, you can have every single thing you wish, but you must become adept at doing exactly as I tell you. Bear in mind that this whole theme is as old as the universe. The only thing I do is to give you what may be considered the practical mechanics.

As we all know, *"the proof of the pudding is in the eating,"* and if you have any doubts as to whether or not I am giving you an exact science, try it. The automobile will begin to take shape, you will get the new shoes and the bricks of the mansion will fall into place as though a magical hand has touched them.

I know it, I believe it and it's so.

I take it that most of us have been taught the efficacy of prayer. Think a moment. It's the wish—the prayer—with that reiteration, repetition, tap, tap, tap. Keep in mind that, as I said before, you are appealing to the subconscious—to that all-powerful force behind—that omnipotent power—a supreme intelligence—or whatever you wish to call it.

The Ancients Tapped

It is easier to go with the current than fight against it, but you must harmonize with others, with everything around you.

"No longer let thy breathing only act in concert with the air which surrounds thee, but let thy intelligence also now be in harmony with the intelligence which embraces all things." —THE WORDS OF A GREAT PHILOSOPHER.

It shouldn't be necessary for me to explain that I am suggesting that you put yourself in tune with the very stream of life itself. You who understand will appreciate that nature provides ways and means for all things to grow rightly. Meditate for a moment and you'll realize I am giving truths which many may have forgotten. There's the great fundamental law of compensation which makes all things right.

There's no set rule for doing anything because some of us perform one way and some another, just as two people go across the river—one goes by one bridge and one another—but they both ultimately get to their destination. In other words, after all is said and done, it's results that count, and, if you will make up your mind to exactly what you want and follow the simple rules which are given herein, everything you are after will be yours.

I know it, I believe it and it's so.

After you get a grip on the Power, do not let the results of its usage surprise you.

Miracles will be performed. You will do what previously you thought impossible.

Tell No One

It is not well that you should tell anyone of your wishes or desires—your innermost ambitions. Keep them to yourself, for should some persons learn what you are after they may place obstacles in your way and otherwise attempt to hinder you. Should barriers accidentally fall or be placed in your path, climb over or go around them. Go whistling blithely by.

Remember nothing can stop you but yourself.

I know it, I believe it and it's so.

I also am one of those who believes that all things are relative. To my way of thinking if a man can earn one dollar he can as easily earn ten. If he has two suits of clothes—he can have ten. The only difference is the amount of energy he is willing to expend and this goes for acquiring $100 to $1000 and from then on it is a matter of only adding ciphers. There is no limit as to what a person may do or secure provided he makes up his mind and steadfastly and determinedly moves towards his goal.

"Look within. Within is the fountain of good, and it will ever bubble up, if thou wilt ever dig" —AN ANCIENT SAYING.

Use It Only For Good

As I said under Detonating Caps be careful how you use the Power which is to be yours. It will act as a boomerang and destroy you and everything you hold dear if you use it for evil. Therefore only use it for doing you and others the most Good and bringing Happiness for yourself and those around you.

Do not talk or boast about what you may have done for others or of your good deeds. They will speak for themselves. Just

65

continue to give thanks for the fact that you are on your way—that's enough.

Have You Got It?

What is personality? What is it that, when you get in the presence of another person who has personality, that grips you? What is it that causes you to feel his very presence— that overshadows you? It's nothing more than a dynamic force coupled with willpower which is drawing from that huge reservoir of the subconscious. There are millions of people who have this personality —some say it's natural with them—perhaps it is—but they are unconsciously using this Power. In other words, it's sort of been thrust upon them and when that thing called personality is backed up with willpower, things move.

To my way of thinking selling bonds, books, clothes, insurance, electric service, washing machines, is no different than selling any other commodity—selling yourself or selling ideas. I have found that trying to put over an idea, firstly I have had to believe in the idea —dream it, eat with it, sleep with it—I had to have it with me every minute of the day until it became part of me—the old idea of repetition again—and I know it works in selling commodities. You have got to know what you are talking about and only hard, personal, persistent, intelligent study will enable you to do this.

One more thing, and that is keep informed as to what is going on in the world about you. You never know what a prospect may be interested in and it's sometimes necessary to get his attention for your "break" entirely through irrelevant subjects —that's why I repeat, read the newspapers, current periodicals, and read them thoroughly. I don't mean read every detail of some murder or suicide, but get a digest of the day's news.

Awaken; know what is going on about you.

Tap No.3

Keep step with the world's affairs. The better informed a person, the better he is equipped to get what he wants.

Don't forget that Knowledge is Power—all of you should know that by this time.

"He who knows others is clever, but he who knows himself is enlightened."
—FROM THE SAYINGS OF A WISE ORIENTAL.

Increase your knowledge and the scope of your activities will be enlarged and the desire for greater things—larger things, will come automatically and, as they do, the things which you previously thought you wanted will become to your mind trivial and will be disregarded, which is another way of saying that you ultimately will hitch your wagon to a star and, when you do, you'll move with lightning-like speed.

Study, learn and work. Develop a keenness of observation. Step on the gas. Become alive for yourself and you'll pass it on to the other fellow. Get confidence, enthusiasm and you'll set up like vibrations all around you and that's the theory of all life—as old as the world itself. Like begets like—a laugh brings a laugh—a good deed calls for a good deed—riches beget riches, love, love— and so on.

The old law of attraction stated in Ampere's theory of electrical magnetism is: *"Parallel currents in the same direction attract one another"*—and when you are out of tune and antagonistic you put others out of tune and make them antagonistic because: *"Parallel currents in opposite directions repel one another."*

Wishbones Need Backbones

However, don't get the thought that I have given you an oversize wishbone which will enable you to sit down and, by talking to yourself, through the idea of repetition, get what you want, because it will never work. You have got to have the wishbone backed up with a backbone and that isn't all—the wishbone and the backbone must be coordinated and synchronized to a point where they are running in perfect harmony, and when they are in tune, you will find personality developing.

I take it that all of us have admired that intense type of person. I mean by that, one whose shoulders are back, whose chest is out, whose head is up and whose eyes are alert. It is easy to pick out in any organization those whose feet lag, whose shoulders droop, whose chins sag and whose eyes are a blank. Drifters, loafers, quitters. First measure yourself. Then study those with whom you are associated and you can tell at almost a glance those who will make progress and those doomed to failure.

Every physical movement tells a story—each marks your personality. Take another good look at yourself in the mirror and probe again and again. You know whether you've got it or not. If not, make up your mind to get it—you can and you will if you make up your mind.

The Eyes Have "It"

If you will develop that intensity of purpose, determination to get ahead, shortly that determination will show in your eyes. You have heard people say that a certain person has a penetrating gaze—that he looks right through one. What is it? Nothing more than that fire from within—intensity—or whatever you wish to call it, which means that the person who has that gaze usually gets what he wants. Remember the eyes are the windows of the soul. Look at the photographs of successful men—study their eyes and you will find that every one of them has that intensity; therefore, I say, let it be reflected in the way you walk, in the way you carry yourself and it will not be long before people will feel your presence when you walk through a crowd—and an individual prospect will feel that personality when you talk with him.

All of this is to explain that it takes an affirmative type to make progress and the things I have pointed out may be utilized to develop you into an affirmative type. The negative type is sunk before he starts. Nature takes care of these situations through the old law of the survival of the fittest. We know what happened in the days of Sparta when children were put on their own at a baby age and only those who survived were given further chance. A negative type is a quitter, or, another way, a quitter is a negative type and, while there is no point to going around hitting everybody on the nose just to start something, always remember it's poor business to let yourself be put on the defensive as that is a negative sign. The person who won't be licked can't be licked. If you are taken unawares and suddenly put on the defensive, snap out of it. Take the offensive because if you remain on the defensive, you are beaten.

Every Day—in Every Way

Of course, to bring about this intensity of being, it's necessary to be in good health. I do not claim that the power of will is a cure-all to mend broken legs and all that sort of thing, but I do know that constant application of the theory herein advanced will aid a person in ill health. All of you have heard of Dr. Emil Coué, the Frenchman, who was in this country a few years ago, telling people they could cure themselves if they would adopt his plan. His idea was that you should say to yourself—*"Every day, in every way, I am getting better and better."* Just ponder over that for a minute.

There was nothing new in that idea, any more than there is in the ideas which I put forth. Simply another way of expressing the whole scheme—reiteration, repetition—keeping uppermost in your mind all the time what you want and which positive thoughts, in turn, are passed on to the subconscious mind—the wonder thing.

Think health, wealth and happiness and they will all be yours. It cannot be otherwise.

We all know of people who are continually talking about backaches, headaches or some other kind of aches. They harp on them and the first thing they know, with that reiteration, the aches become realities. If you have such an ache or pain there is no point to talking about it; neither is there any point to talking about your worries, your troubles. Do not talk about them. Do not think about them. Then they will not be in your mind. It is the repetition that keeps them there. Shift your gears—reverse the process. Get away from the negative side and become an affirmative type—think affirmatively and the first thing you know your aches, worries and troubles will disappear.

"If thou art pained by any external thing, it is not this thing which disturbs thee, but thy own judgment about it. And it is in thy power to wipe out this judgment now. But if anything in thy own disposition gives thee pain, who hinders thee from correcting thy opinion?" —PHILOSOPHY OF THE AGES.

Are You in Reverse?

When a train roars across the track in front of you, you put on the brakes of your automobile, throw the gears into neutral and idle your engine—you are on your way again just as soon as the train passes but you certainly do not throw your gears into reverse and go backwards.

Compare yourself to the gears of your automobile. In reverse place all fears, worries, troubles, aches and pains. And when things go wrong simply put on the brakes, idle your engine until you can clearly see the road ahead. In high is everything you desire, health, wealth, happiness—success. No power in the world except your hand can put the gears of your automobile in reverse. If your own gears get in reverse remember you alone put them there. Erect a steel wall on the right side of the reverse gear, close the doors of yesterday and you will have to shift from low into high and stay there.

"We are living in a great crisis in human history. There is unlimited need for boldness and courage, but there is no occasion for dismay. On the one hand there is the way to such achievements, to such wealth and happiness as mankind has never before known.... life, even as we know it now, tastes very good at times. We spoil it a lot for ourselves and each other by fear, follies, hate, bickering, suspicion and anger. There is no need for us to go on spoiling it. We have not the health we might have. We have not a tithe of the happiness we might have. But it is within the power of the human will to change all that."

—H. G. WELLS, ENGLAND'S GREAT MAN OF LETTERS.

Change Gears Now

This power—this vital energy—or whatever it is, is inexhaustible, and it is so easy to use it if you only have the key. I am fully appreciative of the fact that psychologists maintain that few persons really think. It is my hope that this message will cause You to Think. If you dismiss it as so much balderdash, then I shall know that you have never understood or appreciated how the great characters of history whom I have previously mentioned and many others with whom you yourself should be familiar made names for themselves or gained niches in the hall of fame.

Real people—successful people, are those who made themselves and not what others made them. After all, there are only two ways to move, forward and backward—why not forward? Watch the down-and-outer on the street. His whole trouble is lack of positive ideas. If he thinks he is down and out—he is. If he will change his ideas, he will be up and coming. All of us know that.

You can shift your gears if you only realize it. You have been told how to keep out of reverse and it is simply a mechanical process for yourself. Understand and you will always keep your gears in high and move forward.

Believe in Your Goods

A sale is effected by getting a prospect to think as you do and, unless you believe that the thing you are selling is good then, obviously, you can't make the other fellow believe it.

That is just plain common sense—so, for those of you who may be selling keep in mind what I have previously said about knowing your article and selling yourself— that is 99% of the success of selling—the other 1% is leg work contacting the prospect.

You should realize that the bending other people to your will or getting them to do as you wish is simply having them think as you think and that is very easy.

Sell Yourself

Charles M. Schwab said: *"Many of us think of salesmen as people traveling around with sample kits. Instead, we are all salesmen, every day of our lives. We are selling our ideas, our plans, our energies, our enthusiasm to those with whom we come in contact."* So it is with every endeavor, and especially true of selling commodities because you must contact people. And when I say contact, I mean contacting them face-to-face.

The day of order taking is gone and it is only the persons who have got it in them who are to succeed now—all the others will sink. You cannot beat a fundamental law—*"the survival of the fittest."* Therefore, forget about order taking and keep in mind the only way you can close a sale is to make the prospect think as you think—the best way is in face-to-face contact—you have got to be in his presence—you have got to see his reactions—*"the old law of cause and effect"*—and you have got to adapt yourself to the conditions as they confront you with that individual prospect.

Follow Your Hunches

If you are intent on making a sale—and you must be if you are going to succeed—keep in mind my theme; the subconscious mind will be giving you ideas, hunches, inspirations, a perfect flood of them, which will guide you correctly. They will point out the way to get into a busy man's presence—into the privacy of his very self and, when you get there, stand on both feet.

Be alert. Make him feel your personality. Know what you are talking about. Be enthusiastic. Don't quail.

You are just as good as he is and, besides, you may have something which he hasn't and that is utmost confidence, utmost faith in the article you are selling. On the other hand, if he is a success he also has personality—therefore be sure to put the contact on a fifty-fifty basis. Do not belittle him—do not let him belittle you. Meet on common ground. Make him like you and when he likes you and you him, success is on its way. Remember you are going to sell him.

There is strength in teamwork. The *esprit de corps* pounded into those of us who were in the army made the American forces what they were—and it's the *esprit de corps,* teamwork, determination to move forward which will shove us along. If this is accepted in the spirit in which it is given; put into execution, you will be unbeatable. And by getting in tune and getting others on the track, the world is yours.

"When fear rules the will, nothing can be done, but when a man casts fear out of his mind the world becomes his oyster. To lose a bit of money is nothing but to lose hope— to lose nerve and ambition—that is what makes men cripples." —HERBERT N. CASSON.

Ascertain exactly what you want and use the mechanics given and you will discover more gates open for you than you ever dreamed existed. I am not interested in any prophetic explanations—I am interested in results. A light will dawn upon you and you will see clearly ahead how to achieve what you are after. The same principles, the same methods can be successfully applied to any line.

The ability to accomplish anything in a convincing fashion depends entirely upon the degree of expert knowledge which you possess coupled with that intensity of purpose. Read and study, practice, practice, tap, tap, tap.

Open the Door

Before closing I should tell you that the conscious mind must be placed in a receptive condition to get the ideas from the subjective or subconscious. Of course, we all know it is the conscious mind which reasons, which weighs, which calculates— the subconscious mind does not do any of these things—it simply passes on ideas to the conscious mind.

Relax and Tap

You have heard a lot of people say; "play your hunches"—what are those hunches? Where do they come from? They come from the workings of the subconscious mind. Psychologists tell us—you will soon understand the reason—that to put the human mind in a receptive condition you must relax. If you have ever laid on the massage table and been told by the masseur to relax then you know what I mean. Let the body go limp. If you have trouble at first, try it with your arm—both arms—both legs, until the whole body is relaxed and the mind automatically will relax. When that is accomplished concentrate on what you want —then hunches come. Grab them; execute them as the little voice tells you. Do not reason or argue, but do as you are told and do it immediately.

You will understand what psychologists, mystics and students mean when they tell you to stop, relax—**Think of nothing**— when you wish to draw on the subconscious and have the little inner voice speak. As you further progress you will also begin to realize what the seers of the East had in mind when they said: *"Become at ease, meditate, go into the great silence, continue to meditate and your problems will fade into nothingness."*

The road ahead will become illuminated and your burdens will fall away one by one. Is there anything clearer than "Pilgrim's Progress?" My message is no different than that which was conveyed there—only, as I said before—I put it to you in perhaps different words.

The Mysterious Nothingness

The late Thomas A. Edison explaining his success of inventing said: *"I begin by using my accumulated knowledge but most of my inventions are completed with Ideas which flash into my mind out of thin air."*

Fred Ott and Charles Dally, associated with Mr. Edison for more than 50 years, solved the secret of making synthetic rubber. I quote from a newspaper story dated October 21, 1931: *"On Monday, he (Mr. Edison), started to sink into a stupor. But Dally and Ott were still pounding doggedly (determinedly, concentrating, tap, tap, tap) at their experiments. And on Tuesday night the solution flashed out of the mysterious nothingness."*

The little voice spoke—just like it always does when you make up your mind what you want and when you go after it.

If your own little inner voice suggests that you ask for something, do not be backward about asking. You have nothing to fear. The other person will never help unless he knows your wishes so you must ask.

Accept the theory advanced herein and practice intelligently and the voice will speak just like it did for Edison, Ott, Dally and thousands of others, and you will get results—all will be yours.

In Julius Caesar, Cassius, he of the lean and hungry look, talking to Brutus, of the Roman Emperor's power, said:

"The fault, dear Brutus, is not in our stars, but in Ourselves that we are underlings."

As you know, William Shakespeare wrote that, and he himself arose above the commonplace by using this Power.

Who is to Blame?

If you are timid, backward, in a rut and an underling, it is because of yourself. Blame not the stars. Blame not society. Blame not the world. Blame Yourself. Again I say, change
gears. Put them in High and Begin to Move.

Grip Tightly

Some people not thoroughly understanding may say that you are conceited, self-centered, or selfish but care not what they say. Those are the scoffers—those who would put rocks in your road and otherwise impede your progress. Those who understand will be helpful—they will be eager to serve you. The intelligent ones will begin to study you to determine what you have that they haven't and try to learn your secret.

I have given you a grip on it; hold it to you tightly and start moving forward.

George Jean Nathan, one of America's foremost critics, in a compilation of *"Living*

Philosophies" declares he has never known a man who succeeded in life in a material way who did not think of himself first, last and all the time. Naturally I don't know just how Nathan meant that but I am sure he did not mean that a successful man is selfish to the point where he isn't helpful to others because if you follow the theme as I have outlined it and get on the road to success you will not be led to act ruthlessly.

Service Pays Dividends

As a matter of fact, the exact opposite is true because you will find that you will wish to do charitable things, good things for other people, performing services involving the throwing out of crumbs as it were, and your willingness to do something for the other fellow will bring about a willingness on his part to do something for you. There is nothing selfish about this—it's just a matter of cause and effect. Remember Ampere's laws of attraction. *Like begets like.* When you perform a service you will be paid huge dividends. There is no mystery about it, it's just so.

"I am the master of my fate, I am the captain of my soul."

—HENLEY.

Practice Tap Tap

If this has registered with you in any particular, then I've accomplished something. Read it again carefully and read it again a week from now and keep it to read again. If you'll put into practice the ideas offered you'll soon learn I've given you truths as old as man himself. They've always worked and they always will. Use the mechanics of my system. Make them a part of your daily life and you'll succeed. If you're in earnest with yourself you'll find the whole scheme very simple. Practice, practice—tap, tap, tap—Believe, have Faith and you'll get the golden key to all—yourself.

If you have read this book understandingly you will appreciate the tremendous power which lies in the science of thought repetition and positive action. You can, by the repetition of the same thought, "tap" yourself upward or downward—dependent on whether you have depressed or constructive thoughts. By voicing your thoughts intelligently and convincingly you can, by suggestion, "tap" others up or down, so it behooves you to exercise great care that you do not misuse your POWER.

Fill your mind with creative thoughts and then act as the ideas come to you. Remember: Every thought kept ever constant leads to action. So keep this book and reread it as frequently as possible. Tap —tap—tap.

T.N.T.—It rocks the earth!

Here, there—everywhere.

If you believe it, It is so.

"The more you spread it (your message) the greater will become the service you are rendering to your fellow men."

—PAUL R. KELTY, *Editor,* THE OREGONIAN.
Portland, Or.

Many others, believing that great good must follow, urged me to get my message circulated and this little book is the result. I know what it has done; I know what it will do when passed on to others.

You have friends and acquaintances who are depressed, despondent, in ill health, worried over financial affairs, whose worlds are topsy-turvy; dissatisfied with their lot in life —lost in the wilderness. You may perform a great service by having them read T. N. T. and they need never know that you were responsible for their receiving it.

WE HAVE BOOK RECOMMENDATIONS
FOR YOU

**The Power of Your Subconscious Mind by Joseph Murphy
[UNABRIDGED] (Audio CD)**

**Think and Grow Rich [MP3 AUDIO]
[UNABRIDGED]
by Napoleon Hill, Jason McCoy (Narrator) (Audio CD)**

**As a Man Thinketh [UNABRIDGED]
by James Allen, Jason McCoy (Narrator) (Audio CD)**

BN Publishing

Improving People's Life

www.bnpublishing.com

Printed in the United States
109015LV00001B/56/A